Mastering

DISCIPLINE
and
SELF CONTROL

Strategies for Achieving Success

AVERY JAMESON

TABLE OF CONTENTS

Introduction

Two of the most effective tools we have for achieving success and happiness in our lives are discipline and self-control. They serve as the cornerstone for all other accomplishments, both personal and professional. We are at the whim of our impulses, emotions, and outside situations if we lack self-control and discipline. We may have ambitions and goals, but without the capacity to maintain concentration, put in significant effort, and make challenging decisions, we will never be able to accomplish them.

They are also the most powerful tools that we can use to achieve success and happiness in our lives. They are the foundation upon which all other personal and professional achievements are built. Without discipline and self-control, we are at the mercy of our impulses, emotions, and external circumstances. We may have goals and aspirations, but without the ability to stay focused, work hard, and make difficult choices, we will never be able to reach them.

In this book, I will explore the importance of discipline and self-control in our lives and offer practical strategies for developing and strengthening these qualities. We will begin by examining the science behind self-control and the ways in which it can be improved. We will then explore the role of discipline in achieving long-term success and happiness, and the ways in which it can be developed and maintained.

I will draw on the most recent findings in psychology, neurology, and behavior change throughout the book to offer practical suggestions and examples of how self-control and discipline can be used in a range of situations. The guidelines and tactics presented in this book will assist you in overcoming challenges, maintaining concentration, and achieving your objectives, whether your goals are to better your health, relationships, or profession.

So, come along on this journey of self-discovery and personal development with me if you're ready to take charge of your life and realize your full potential. Let's start the process of developing self-control and discipline so that we can all achieve the success and happiness we deserve.

Chapter 1

Understanding Discipline and Self-Control

Discipline and self-control are important traits that are highly valued in many areas of life, such as education, career, relationships, and personal growth. They enable individuals to make progress towards their goals and overcome obstacles that may arise along the way. Let's take a closer look at the definitions of discipline and self-control, their differences, and the benefits of developing these two traits.

Definition of Discipline

Discipline is a learned behavior that involves the practice of staying focused on one's goals and taking the necessary steps to achieve them, even when faced with distractions, setbacks, or difficulties. It is characterized by consistency, commitment, and determination. Discipline is not a natural talent, but rather a skill that can be developed and strengthened through practice and persistence.

Discipline is not limited to any particular area of life. It can be applied to any situation where individuals need to set goals, prioritize tasks, and stay on track to achieve them. For example, a student may need discipline to study consistently, a musician may need discipline to practice regularly, and an athlete may need discipline to maintain a rigorous training schedule. Without discipline, it is easy to become distracted, procrastinate, or lose motivation.

Definition of Self-Control

Self-control is the ability to regulate one's thoughts, emotions, and behaviors in a manner that is consistent with one's values and goals. It involves resisting impulses, delaying gratification, and making deliberate choices based on long-term consequences. Self-control is essential for achieving success, maintaining healthy relationships, and managing one's emotions effectively.

Self-control is not an all-or-nothing trait. Rather, it exists on a continuum, and individuals can develop and improve their self-control skills over time. For example, an individual may struggle with impulsive eating or spending habits but may learn to control those impulses through self-reflection, mindfulness, and other techniques.

The Difference between Discipline and Self-Control:

While discipline and self-control are related concepts, there is a subtle difference between them. Discipline refers to the practice of staying focused on one's goals and taking the necessary steps to achieve them. It involves setting priorities, creating habits, and developing a sense of purpose. Self-control, on the other hand, refers to the ability to regulate one's thoughts, emotions, and behaviors. It involves managing impulses, avoiding distractions, and making conscious choices.

In essence, discipline is about creating structure and direction in one's life, while self-control is about managing one's reactions to that structure and direction. Both traits are essential for personal development, but they involve different skills and strategies.

The Benefits of Developing Discipline and Self-Control:

Developing discipline and self-control can have numerous benefits for individuals. Here are some of them:

Achieving Goals: Discipline and self-control are essential for achieving one's goals. Without these traits, it is easy to become distracted, lose motivation, or give up on one's dreams.

Improved Productivity: Discipline and self-control enable individuals to work efficiently and effectively. They help individuals prioritize their tasks, manage their time effectively, and avoid distractions that can hinder productivity.

Better Relationships: Self-control is necessary for building and maintaining healthy relationships. It helps individuals avoid impulsive behaviors that can harm their relationships, and it enables them to communicate effectively and empathetically.

Greater Happiness: Discipline and self-control lead to greater satisfaction and happiness in life. By achieving goals and making progress in various areas of life, individuals experience a sense of fulfillment and contentment.

Improved Mental Health: Developing discipline and self-control can also improve one's mental health. It can reduce stress, anxiety, and depression, and promote a sense of calm and well-being.

Chapter 2

The Psychology of Discipline and Self-Control

Discipline and self-control are fundamental traits that can help us achieve success and accomplish our goals. However, building discipline and self-control is not always easy, and it requires understanding the science behind these traits and the strategies we can use to train our brain to develop them. In this chapter, we will delve deeper into the psychology of discipline and self-control, exploring the research, theories, and practical strategies that can help us develop these essential traits.

The Science Behind Discipline and Self-Control

Discipline and self-control are not simply a matter of willpower or motivation. There is a complex interplay between biology, psychology, and environmental factors that shapes our ability to regulate our behavior and resist impulses. Researchers have identified several key areas of the brain that are involved in self-control, including the prefrontal cortex, anterior cingulate cortex, and the insula.

The prefrontal cortex is the part of the brain that is responsible for decision-making, planning, and self-regulation. It is located at the front of the brain and plays a critical role in our ability to control our behavior and resist impulses. The anterior cingulate cortex is involved in monitoring and regulating our emotions, while the insula is involved in sensing and processing our internal bodily states.

Several studies have shown that the prefrontal cortex is particularly vulnerable to stress, sleep deprivation, and poor nutrition. When we are stressed, tired, or hungry, our prefrontal cortex may not function optimally, which can make it harder for us to control our behavior and make good decisions.

How Our Brain Works and Why We Struggle with Discipline and Self-Control;

To understand the psychology of discipline and self-control, we need to delve into the complex workings of the brain. The brain has two primary systems that are involved in decision-making and self-control: the automatic system and the reflective system.

The automatic system is fast and effortless, and it operates outside of our conscious awareness. It is responsible for our automatic thoughts, emotions, and behaviors, and it is often driven by habit and instinct. The reflective system, on the other hand, is slow and effortful, and it involves conscious thinking and deliberate decision-making.

When we are faced with a situation that requires self-control, both systems are activated. The automatic system may urge us to give in to our impulses, while the reflective system may try to resist those impulses and make a deliberate decision. However, because the automatic system is fast and effortless, it often wins out over the reflective system, particularly when we are stressed, tired, or distracted.

Research has shown that there are several key factors that can influence our ability to exert self-control. These include our emotional state, our level of cognitive load, and our level of motivation. When we are emotionally aroused or stressed, our ability to control our behavior may be compromised. Similarly, when we are overloaded with cognitive tasks, we may have less mental resources available for self-control. Finally, when our motivation is low, we may be less willing to exert the effort needed for self-control.

Strategies for Training Our Brain to Develop Discipline and Self-Control

While our brain may be wired to favor the automatic system, we can train our brain to develop better discipline and self-control through practice and repetition. Here are some strategies that can help:

Create Structure: Creating structure and routine in our daily lives can help us develop discipline and self-control. By setting specific goals, prioritizing tasks, and creating habits, we can train our brain to focus on what is important and resist distractions. For example, we might set aside a specific time each day for exercise, or we might prioritize our most important tasks for the day before checking email or social media.

Practice mindfulness: Being fully present in the moment, without distraction or judgment, is the practice of mindfulness. According to research, mindfulness can enhance self-control by lowering stress, enhancing emotional control, and enhancing concentration. Try setting aside a short period of time each day to concentrate on your breathing and notice your thoughts and sensations without passing judgment.

Use Implementation Intentions: Implementation intentions are specific plans that we create to guide our behavior in a given situation. For example, we might create an implementation intention like "If I feel the urge to check social media, I will take a 5-minute break instead." By creating specific plans for how we will respond to different situations, we can train our brain to automatically choose the more disciplined option.

Build Self-Awareness: Developing self-awareness can help us better understand our emotions, thoughts, and behaviors, and can help us identify the triggers that lead us to lose self-control. To build self-awareness, try journaling or reflecting on your experiences to identify patterns and triggers in your behavior.

Use Positive Reinforcement: Positive reinforcement involves rewarding ourselves for positive behavior, which can help us build motivation and reinforce good habits. For example, we might reward ourselves with a favorite treat or activity after completing a challenging task. By using positive reinforcement, we can train our brain to associate discipline and self-control with positive outcomes.

Chapter 3

The Power of Habits in Developing Discipline and Self-Control

Habits play a powerful role in our lives, shaping our behavior and influencing the choices we make on a daily basis. Whether we realize it or not, our habits can either support or hinder our efforts to develop discipline and self-control. In this chapter, we will explore the science of habits and learn how to create new habits to support our goals, as well as how to break bad habits that hold us back.

How Habits Are Formed and How They Affect Our Behavior

Habits are formed through a process called "habituation," in which the brain creates neural pathways that make certain behaviors automatic and effortless. When we perform a behavior repeatedly, our brain begins to recognize the pattern and creates a shortcut, allowing us to perform the behavior without much conscious thought. Over time, these neural pathways become stronger and more ingrained, making the behavior more automatic and less subject to conscious control.

The power of habits lies in their ability to shape our behavior without requiring much effort or conscious decision-making. This can be both a blessing and a curse, as habits can either support or hinder our efforts to develop discipline and self-control. For example, if we have a habit of checking our phone every few minutes, this can distract us from important tasks and make it harder to stay focused and disciplined. On the other hand, if we have a habit of exercising every morning, this can make it easier to stick to a healthy routine and build self-control.

Creating New Habits to Support Discipline and Self-Control

Creating new habits to support discipline and self-control requires a deliberate and intentional approach. Here are some strategies for building new habits:

Start with a small, manageable change: It can be tempting to try to make big changes all at once, but this can often lead to overwhelm and failure. Instead, it's important to start small and focus on creating one new habit at a time. For example, if you want to start exercising more regularly, you might start with a goal of walking for 10 minutes each day.

Be consistent: Habits are formed through consistent behavior over time, so it's important to create a daily routine that supports your goals and stick to it, even on days when you don't feel motivated. By consistently practicing discipline and self-control, you can train your brain to make these behaviors automatic and effortless.

Use positive reinforcement: Positive reinforcement involves rewarding yourself for positive behavior, which can help you build motivation and reinforce good habits. For example, you might reward yourself with a favorite treat or activity after completing a challenging task. By using positive reinforcement, you can train your brain to associate discipline and self-control with positive outcomes.

Track your progress: Keeping track of your progress can be a powerful motivator for building new habits. Whether you use a journal, a habit-tracking app, or another method, tracking your progress can help you see the impact of your efforts and keep you accountable to your goals.

Breaking Bad Habits That Hinder Our Progress: Breaking bad habits can be challenging, but it's an important step in developing discipline and self-control. Here are some strategies for breaking bad habits:

Identify the trigger: Bad habits often have a trigger that sets them in motion. For example, if you have a habit of snacking late at night, the trigger might be feeling bored or stressed. By identifying the trigger, you can take steps to avoid it or replace the habit with a healthier alternative.

Make a strategy: You need a strategy to break a harmful habit. You may decide to turn off notifications or leave your phone in a different room during work hours, for instance, if you wish to cease checking your phone during that time.

Use substitution: Substituting a bad habit with a healthier alternative can be an effective way to break the habit. For example, if you have a habit of snacking on junk food, you might substitute it with healthier snacks like fruits or nuts.

Use negative reinforcement: Negative reinforcement involves creating a negative consequence for bad behavior, which can help you break the habit. For example, if you have a habit of procrastinating, you might create a consequence like having to do an extra hour of work the next day.

Get support: Breaking a bad habit can be difficult, so it's important to get support from others. Whether you join a support group, work with a coach, or simply talk to a friend, having support can make the process easier and more effective.

Build momentum: Building momentum by starting small can be a helpful strategy for developing new habits. Instead of trying to make a huge change all at once, start with a small habit that you can stick to and gradually build on it over time. For example, if you want to start a daily exercise routine, start with just a few minutes a day and gradually increase the time and intensity.

Use positive reinforcement: Positive reinforcement involves rewarding good behavior, which can help to reinforce new habits. For example, if you want to develop a habit of reading every day, you might reward yourself with a treat or a fun activity after you have completed your reading.

Track your progress: Keeping track of your progress can help to motivate you and keep you accountable. Whether you use a journal, an app, or a habit tracker, tracking your progress can help you see how far you have come and give you a sense of accomplishment.

Be patient: Developing new habits and breaking bad habits takes time and patience. Expecting results right away is unrealistic, and you shouldn't be too hard on yourself if you make mistakes. Instead, emphasize progress rather than perfection and acknowledge little victories along the way.

Chapter 4

Strategies for Developing Discipline and Self-Control

Discipline and self-control are essential qualities for achieving success in all areas of life. However, developing these qualities requires conscious effort and the application of specific strategies. In this chapter, we will explore two important strategies for developing discipline and self-control: goal setting and planning, and techniques for resisting temptation and delaying gratification.

Goal Setting and Planning for Success

The first step in developing discipline and self-control is to set clear goals and create a plan for achieving them. Goal setting provides direction and focus, and can help to motivate you towards action. Without clear goals, it is easy to become distracted or aimless, which can hinder your progress.

To set effective goals, it is important to make them specific, measurable, achievable, relevant, and time-bound. This framework, known as SMART goals, can help you create goals that are realistic and meaningful. For example, instead of setting a goal to "exercise more," you might set a SMART goal to "go for a 30-minute walk every day after work for the next 30 days." This goal is specific, measurable, achievable, relevant, and time-bound, making it more likely that you will achieve it.

Once you have set your goals, it is important to create a plan for achieving them. This plan should include specific actions and milestones that will help you make progress towards your goals. It can also be helpful to identify potential obstacles and come up with strategies for overcoming them. By creating a plan and sticking to it, you can develop the discipline and self-control needed to achieve your goals.

Techniques for Resisting Temptation and Delaying Gratification

One of the biggest challenges in developing discipline and self-control is resisting the temptation for immediate pleasure or gratification in favor of a larger, long-term reward. This challenge is particularly evident in areas like diet and exercise, where it can be difficult to resist the temptation of unhealthy foods or skip a workout in favor of a more leisurely activity.

To overcome this challenge, there are several techniques you can use to resist temptation and delay gratification:

Mindfulness: Practicing mindfulness can help you become more aware of your thoughts and emotions, and can help you develop the self-awareness and self-regulation needed for discipline and self-control. When faced with temptation, take a moment to pause, breathe, and become aware of your thoughts and feelings.

Positive self-talk: Self-talk refers to the internal dialogue you have with yourself. By using positive self-talk, you can motivate yourself towards action and resist the temptation for immediate gratification. For example, instead of saying "I can't resist this chocolate cake," try saying "I am choosing to prioritize my health and wellbeing by choosing a healthier snack."

Delayed gratification exercises: Practicing delayed gratification exercises can help you build the skill of resisting temptation and delaying gratification. One popular exercise is the marshmallow test, where participants are asked to resist eating a marshmallow for a period of time in exchange for a larger reward. By practicing these exercises, you can strengthen your ability to resist temptation and delay gratification.

Accountability: Having accountability partners or systems in place can help you stay on track towards your goals. This can include sharing your goals with friends or family, joining a support group, or hiring a coach or mentor. Knowing that others are aware of your goals and progress can provide an extra level of motivation and accountability.

Creating a supportive environment: Your environment can have a significant impact on your behavior and ability to develop discipline and self-control. Creating a supportive environment can include removing temptations, surrounding yourself with like-minded individuals, or setting up systems to make your desired behavior easier to accomplish. For example, if your goal is to exercise more, you can remove distractions by turning off your phone during your workout, and setting out your workout clothes the night before to make it easier to get started.

Mindfulness and meditation: Practicing mindfulness and meditation can help you develop greater self-awareness and improve your ability to regulate your behavior. Mindfulness involves being present in the moment and fully engaged in your actions, thoughts, and feelings. By practicing mindfulness, you can become more aware of your thoughts and emotions, and learn to recognize when you are feeling triggered or tempted. This can help you to resist impulsive actions and make more intentional choices.

Self-compassion: Developing self-compassion can also be a powerful tool for developing discipline and self-control. Self-compassion involves treating yourself with kindness, understanding, and acceptance, rather than being overly critical or harsh. When you make mistakes or experience setbacks, self-compassion can help you to stay motivated and committed to your goals, rather than giving up or becoming discouraged.

Gratitude: Cultivating a sense of gratitude can also be an effective strategy for developing discipline and self-control. By focusing on what you are grateful for, you can shift your attention away from temptations or distractions, and stay focused on your goals. Gratitude can also help you to maintain a positive outlook and stay motivated in the face of challenges or setbacks.

Continual learning and growth: Finally, it's important to recognize that developing discipline and self-control is an ongoing process that requires continual learning and growth. This can involve seeking out new information and resources, trying new strategies and techniques, and being open to feedback and guidance from others. By maintaining a growth mindset and staying committed to your goals, you can continue to develop greater discipline and self-control over time.

Procrastination is the enemy of productivity, and it affects us all. We often find ourselves putting off important tasks until the last minute, which can cause stress and anxiety. This is where discipline and self-control come into play. In order to overcome procrastination and build consistency, we must first understand what causes it and then develop strategies to combat it. In this article, we will explore these strategies and how they relate to the book "Discipline and Self-Control."

Understanding Procrastination

Procrastination is the act of delaying or putting off tasks that need to be done. It can be caused by a variety of factors, including fear, anxiety, and lack of motivation. For some people, procrastination is a habit that they have developed over time, while for others, it may be a symptom of an underlying mental health issue such as depression or ADHD.

The Effects of Procrastination

Procrastination can have several negative effects on our lives. It can cause us to miss deadlines, feel overwhelmed, and experience a decline in productivity. Procrastination can also lead to feelings of guilt, shame, and self-doubt, which can further exacerbate the problem. Ultimately, procrastination can prevent us from reaching our goals and living up to our full potential.

Strategies for Overcoming Procrastination

Set Clear Goals and Priorities: One of the main reasons why we procrastinate is that we are unsure of what we need to do. By setting clear goals and priorities, we can eliminate this uncertainty and focus on what needs to be done. When setting goals, it's important to be specific and measurable. For example, instead of saying "I want to write a book," say "I want to write a 500-page book on self-discipline and self-control by the end of the year." This way, you have a clear target to aim for, and you can measure your progress along the way.

Break Tasks into Smaller Chunks

Another reason why we procrastinate is that we feel overwhelmed by the task at hand. By breaking tasks into smaller chunks, we can make them more manageable and less daunting. This strategy is known as "chunking," and it involves dividing a larger task into smaller, more achievable tasks. For example, instead of writing a 500-page book in one go, you could break it down into chapters or sections.

Use a Timer or Schedule

Using a timer or schedule can help you stay on track and avoid procrastination. Set a timer for a specific amount of time, and work on a task until the timer goes off. This technique is known as the Pomodoro Technique, and it involves working in short, focused bursts. Alternatively, you could use a schedule to plan out your day or week, and allocate specific times for each task.

Eliminate Distractions

Distractions are a major contributor to procrastination. To overcome this, you need to identify what distracts you and take steps to eliminate them. This could involve turning off your phone or email notifications, closing unnecessary tabs on your computer, or working in a quiet, distraction-free environment.

Hold Yourself Accountable

Accountability is key to overcoming procrastination and building consistency. Hold yourself accountable by setting deadlines and making a commitment to yourself to complete tasks on time. You could also enlist the help of a friend or colleague to hold you accountable and provide support and encouragement.

How Discipline and Self-Control Contribute to Overcoming Procrastination

Discipline and self-control are essential qualities for overcoming procrastination and building consistency. By developing discipline and self-control, you can better manage your time, stay focused on your goals, and resist the urge to procrastinate.

Discipline, on the other hand, can be developed through goal-setting and consistency. By setting clear goals and establishing a routine, we can create a sense of structure and accountability that can help us stay on track and avoid procrastination. The author may also discuss how discipline can be strengthened through positive reinforcement and self-reward. For example, after completing a task on time, we can reward ourselves with something we enjoy, such as a favorite treat or activity.

By combining these strategies with the principles of discipline and self-control, we can overcome procrastination and build consistency in our lives. This can have a profound impact on our personal and professional success, as we become more productive, focused, and self-assured.

Chapter 5

Maintaining Discipline and Self-Control: The Importance of Accountability and Support

Discipline and self-control are essential qualities that can help individuals achieve their goals and overcome obstacles. However, maintaining discipline and self-control can be challenging, especially when faced with distractions and temptations. In this chapter, we will explore the importance of accountability and support in maintaining discipline and self-control.

Accountability

Accountability refers to taking responsibility for one's actions and being answerable to others for those actions. Being accountable to someone can help individuals stay focused and motivated. For example, if someone has committed to completing a task by a certain deadline, they are more likely to follow through if they know that others are counting on them. This sense of accountability can also help individuals overcome procrastination and stay on track with their goals.

In terms of maintaining discipline and self-control, accountability can be a powerful tool. By sharing their goals and progress with others, individuals can create a sense of accountability that can motivate them to stay on track. This could involve sharing goals with a friend, family member, or mentor, or joining a support group or accountability partnership. In these settings, individuals can receive encouragement, feedback, and accountability to help them maintain their discipline and self-control.

Support

In addition to accountability, support is also crucial in maintaining discipline and self-control. Support can come in many forms, including emotional support, practical support, and social support. Emotional support involves having someone to talk to and rely on during times of stress or difficulty. Practical support involves receiving assistance with tasks and responsibilities, such as childcare or household chores. Social support involves being part of a network of individuals who share similar goals and can provide motivation and encouragement.

Support is essential because it helps individuals feel connected, valued, and motivated. When individuals feel supported, they are more likely to maintain their discipline and self-control. For example, if someone is trying to quit smoking, having a support group of individuals who have successfully quit can provide inspiration and motivation to stick with it.

Certainly! Self-reflection and self-assessment are essential practices for developing discipline and self-control. They require an individual to take an honest and introspective look at their thoughts, emotions, and behaviors to better understand themselves and identify areas for growth and improvement.

In the context of discipline and self-control, self-reflection involves reflecting on one's thoughts and behaviors to identify the underlying causes of unwanted impulses and habits. This requires taking a step back and observing oneself without judgment. For example, an individual may reflect on their daily routines and identify times when they are most susceptible to distractions or temptations, such as checking their phone first thing in the morning or indulging in unhealthy snacks in the afternoon. By gaining a deeper understanding of these triggers, they can develop strategies for managing them more effectively.

Self-assessment, on the other hand, involves setting specific goals and evaluating one's own progress towards achieving them. This process requires an individual to be honest with themselves about their strengths and weaknesses, and to develop a plan for improvement. For example, an individual may set a goal to wake up earlier each day to allow for more time to exercise or complete work tasks. By tracking their progress towards this goal, they can stay accountable to themselves and adjust their approach as needed.

Both self-reflection and self-assessment require a certain level of discipline and self-control to be effective. They require an individual to take ownership of their actions and be willing to make changes to achieve their desired outcomes. It's important to approach these practices with a growth mindset, recognizing that failure and setbacks are an inevitable part of the process. By using self-reflection and self-assessment as tools for personal growth and development, individuals can develop the discipline and self-control needed to achieve their goals and reach their full pot

Celebrating progress and rewarding success are essential components of developing discipline and self-control. These practices provide a positive reinforcement for desired behaviors, making it easier to maintain consistency and motivation towards achieving goals. In this write-up, we will explore the importance of celebrating progress and rewarding success in relation to discipline and self-control, and offer some practical tips for implementing these practices into your life.

Firstly, celebrating progress and rewarding success help to establish a positive feedback loop for desired behaviors. When we celebrate our progress towards a goal or reward ourselves for a job well done, we create positive associations with the behavior that led to that success. This positive reinforcement makes it easier to continue the desired behavior in the future, as it creates an internal motivation to continue pursuing the goal. This is particularly important when developing discipline and self-control, as these are qualities that require consistent effort and practice to develop.

One way to celebrate progress is to break down larger goals into smaller milestones, and celebrate each milestone as it is achieved. For example, if your goal is to exercise for 30 minutes every day, you could celebrate each week that you successfully complete this goal by treating yourself to a small reward, such as a relaxing bubble bath or a favorite snack. This not only provides a positive reinforcement for the behavior, but also helps to create a sense of momentum towards the larger goal.

Similarly, rewarding success can be a powerful motivator for continuing desired behaviors. When we reward ourselves for a job well done, we create a positive association with the effort we put in, making it easier to maintain that effort in the future. This is particularly important for developing discipline and self-control, as these qualities require consistent effort and practice to maintain.

When it comes to rewarding success, it's important to choose rewards that are meaningful to you and aligned with your goals. For example, if your goal is to save money, a reward of a shopping spree may not be the best choice. Instead, you could reward yourself with a small treat, such as a fancy coffee or a night out with friends, that is within your budget and consistent with your values.

Another important aspect of celebrating progress and rewarding success is the role that social support can play. Having a support system in place can make it easier to stay motivated and on track towards your goals. This can include friends, family members, or even online communities that share your goals and interests. By sharing your progress and successes with others, you create a sense of accountability and positive reinforcement that can help you stay on track towards achieving your goals.

Finally, it's important to keep in mind that celebrating progress and rewarding success are not just about achieving a specific outcome, but also about the process of growth and self-improvement. By focusing on the effort and progress you make towards your goals, rather than solely on the end result, you create a sense of satisfaction and pride in your accomplishments. This can help you maintain a positive attitude towards the process of self-improvement, even when faced with setbacks or challenges.

In summary, celebrating progress and rewarding success are essential components of developing discipline and self-control. By creating a positive reinforcement for desired behaviors, establishing meaningful rewards, and cultivating a supportive community, we can make it easier to maintain consistent effort towards achieving our goals. It's important to keep in mind that these practices are not just about achieving a specific outcome, but also about the process of growth and self-improvement. By focusing on the effort and progress we make towards our goals, we can maintain a positive attitude towards the process of self-improvement and achieve our full potential.

Summary

In summary, discipline and self-control are critical skills that are necessary for personal growth and success in various aspects of life. These skills require consistent effort and practice to develop and maintain, but the rewards of having strong discipline and self-control can be immense. In this conclusion, we will recap the importance of discipline and self-control, provide encouragement to act and develop these critical skills, and offer resources for further learning and growth.

Discipline and self-control are essential for achieving our goals and aspirations. Without these qualities, it is easy to become distracted or discouraged and give up on our dreams. By developing discipline and self-control, we can create a sense of purpose and direction in our lives, and work towards our goals with focus and determination.

One of the most important aspects of developing discipline and self-control is to start with small, manageable changes. It can be tempting to try to change everything at once, but this often leads to frustration and burnout. Instead, it's better to start with one or two areas where you would like to improve and focus your efforts there. Over time, as you build confidence and momentum, you can expand your efforts to other areas.

Another key to developing discipline and self-control is to establish clear goals and a plan for achieving them. When we have a clear vision of what we want to achieve and a roadmap for getting there, it becomes easier to stay motivated and on track towards our goals. It's also important to set realistic expectations and be patient with ourselves as we work towards our goals.

Remember, developing discipline and self-control is a process, and it takes time and effort to build these qualities.

Encouragement and support are also critical for developing discipline and self-control. Surrounding ourselves with people who encourage us and hold us accountable can make it easier to stay motivated and focused. This can include family members, friends, or even online communities that share our goals and interests. By seeking out these sources of support, we create a sense of accountability and positive reinforcement that can help us stay on track towards achieving our goals.

In conclusion, developing discipline and self-control is essential for personal growth and success. These qualities require consistent effort and practice to develop, but the rewards of having strong discipline and self-control can be immense. By starting with small, manageable changes, establishing clear goals and a plan for achieving them, seeking out support and encouragement, and using resources for further learning and growth, we can develop the discipline and self-control we need to achieve our full potential. So, let us all make a conscious effort to cultivate these qualities in ourselves, and encourage others to do the same. Together, we can create a world where discipline and self-control are celebrated as the key ingredients for success and personal growth.

I hope to see you on the brighter side of life.

Thank you.

www.ingramcontent.com/pod-product-compliance
Lightning Source LLC
Chambersburg PA
CBHW071023260726
48662CB00024B/1810